Mosque

Lisa Magloff

Muslims at daily prayer

Word list

Look out for these words as you go through the book. They are shown using CAPITALS.

ARABIC This is the language spoken in countries like Saudi Arabia, Yemen, Egypt and Morocco. It is also the language spoken by the first Muslims and the language that the Qur'an was first written in.

CALLIGRAPHY Writing that has been made in a beautiful or fancy way, so that it is also art. The Qur'an is sometimes written in beautiful calligraphy, to show how important it is.

CRESCENT MOON The Crescent Moon is often used as a symbol of Islam. Because the first Muslims lived in the desert, they used the Moon to guide them at night. So, one meaning of the Crescent Moon is to show how God lights and guides a Muslim's way through life.

EID AL-ADHA This is one of the most important celebrations of the Muslim year. It is celebrated with special prayers and a big meal.

EID AL-FITR This is a celebration at the end of the Islamic month of Ramadan. During Ramadan, Muslims do not eat anything between sunrise and sunset.

IMAM The leader of the religious community. Imams are usually people who have studied Islamic law and religion, often at Islamic universities or schools. The imam leads the prayers in the mosque and gives the sermon at the noon prayer on Fridays.

ISLAM The religion followed by Muslims. Islam is an Arabic word which means obedience.

Islam is a set of beliefs and practices. Islamic beliefs include the belief in one God (Allah) and that the prophet Mohammed (pbuh) was God's most recent prophet.

MIHRAB Muslims must always pray facing the city of Mecca. One wall of the prayer hall always faces Mecca, and on this wall is a niche, called the mihrab.

MINBAR A platform, or pulpit, with three or more steps. The imam stands on the minbar to give his Friday sermon. The imam never stands on the top step – that is reserved for the prophet Mohammed (pbuh).

MOSQUE A building where Muslims go to pray and to be part of the Muslim community. Mosques can be large or small, plain or fancy.

MUSLIM A Muslim is a person who follows the Islamic religion. The word Muslim is an Arabic word which means "a person who obeys God". There are more than one billion Muslims around the world.

PRAYER HALL The room in a mosque where people pray. One wall of the prayer hall always faces the direction of Mecca.

PROPHET MOHAMMED (PBUH) The founder of Islam. He was born about fourteen centuries ago near the city of Mecca in what is now Saudi Arabia.

Muslims believe that God sent many messages to the prophet Mohammed (pbuh). The prophet Mohammed (pbuh) then preached these messages to the people around Mecca.

The words peace be unto him, or the abbreviation pbuh, are often placed after the prophet Mohammed's (pbuh) name, to show respect.

QUR'AN The holy book of Islam. Muslims believe that, during his lifetime, the prophet Mohammed (pbuh) received many messages from God. Because the prophet Mohammed (pbuh) could not write, he recited these messages to his followers, who memorised them. During his lifetime and after the prophet Mohammed's (pbuh) death, his followers wrote down the messages in the Qur'an.

SERMON A talk or lecture about a religious subject. In Islam, the sermon is always given by the imam after the noon prayer on Fridays.

UMMA This is an Arabic word which means "worldwide community of Islam". The umma is made up of all the Muslims in the world.

Contents

In this book we use the abbreviation (pbuh) for "peace be unto him", a sign of respect for the prophet Mohammed.

 Be considerate!

When visiting a place of worship, remember that it is sacred to believers and so be considerate to their feelings. It doesn't take a lot of effort – just attitude.

Part of a meeting room in a mosque.

What is a mosque for?

A mosque is a religious building in which Muslims pray.

A **MOSQUE** is a place in which **MUSLIMS** pray. The centre of the mosque is a large hall called the **PRAYER HALL**. You can see this in picture ①.

Muslim prayers involve standing, bowing and kneeling, so there is no need to have chairs. There may, however, be rugs on the floor. This is so people will have a clean place to pray (picture ②).

The prayer hall

The prayer hall is a beautiful room but it does not have any statues or paintings of people, even important people like the **PROPHET MOHAMMED (PBUH)**. This is because **ISLAM** teaches that people must never pray to a statue or image, only to Allah (God).

▶ ① This is a prayer hall in a large mosque. There are no chairs, because prayer involves standing and kneeling. A cleric, or IMAM is shown here preaching from the MINBAR, or pulpit. The wall behind the imam faces the holy city of Mecca.

◀ ② A prayer mat with a beautiful design.

Praying

Many of the special things you see inside the mosque are used in prayer.

Prayer is a necessary part of the Islamic religion. Muslims do not, therefore, ask anything from God when they pray.

Many Muslims pray five times each day. Muslims must wash in a special way before they pray. Then they follow a pattern of prayer which is carried out according to strict rules.

During prayer, Muslims bow, kneel and touch their head to the ground in homage. This cycle of prayer is called a rak'ah (picture ①).

Facing Mecca

Muslims must pray facing the direction of the holiest city which is called Mecca. Mecca is in the Middle Eastern country called Saudi Arabia.

One wall of the prayer hall always faces towards Mecca. You can tell which wall this is because it will have a small niche, called a **MIHRAB** (picture ②). During prayers everyone, including the **IMAM**, faces the mihrab (picture ③).

Some mosques also have a 'pulpit', called a **MINBAR** (picture ①, page 4). Not all mosques have a minbar, so sometimes the imam just stands up in front of the congregation.

▼ ① **Muslims at prayer.**

▼ ② The mihrab may be plain, or it may be decorated with colourful tiles and writing. This mihrab is in a Turkish mosque, so the designs are in a Turkish style. There is usually a clock near the mihrab, to remind people when it is time to pray.

▼▲ ③ Men and women pray behind the same imam but in separate areas. (Below) The main prayer hall where men pray. (Above) There is often a balcony above the prayer hall. This is where women pray.

7

A traditional mosque

Many large mosques have extra features that have special meanings in Islam.

Many mosques around the world are large and have extra features. There is no rule that says what a mosque must look like, but many mosques are designed to look like the mosques built in the early days of Islam (picture ①).

The minaret

One of the things you might notice are some tall towers next to the mosque. These are called minarets.

A long time ago, before clocks and watches, the minaret was used as a high point from which the call to prayer could be shouted over the roof tops. It is the same as ringing bells in a Christian church.

Today, the tradition continues.

The courtyard

Traditional mosques often have a courtyard with running water and are planted with flowers and trees.

The first mosques were in hot, dry places, and this was a cool place for people to gather. Today, people still gather in mosque courtyards to talk or sit quietly.

Muslims believe that heaven contains many beautiful gardens, and so the mosque gardens also help remind people that if they are good Muslims, they will go to heaven.

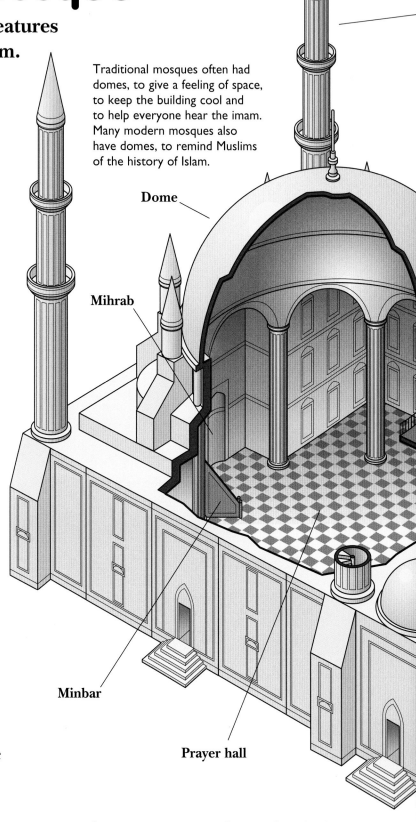

Traditional mosques often had domes, to give a feeling of space, to keep the building cool and to help everyone hear the imam. Many modern mosques also have domes, to remind Muslims of the history of Islam.

Dome

Mihrab

Minbar

Prayer hall

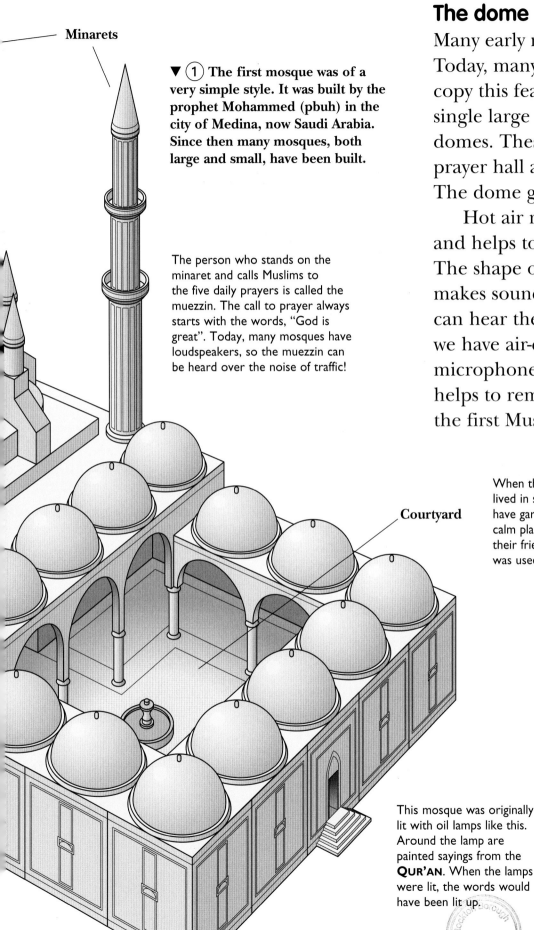

Minarets

▼ ① **The first mosque was of a very simple style. It was built by the prophet Mohammed (pbuh) in the city of Medina, now Saudi Arabia. Since then many mosques, both large and small, have been built.**

The person who stands on the minaret and calls Muslims to the five daily prayers is called the muezzin. The call to prayer always starts with the words, "God is great". Today, many mosques have loudspeakers, so the muezzin can be heard over the noise of traffic!

The dome

Many early mosques had domes. Today, many large mosques still copy this feature, either with a single large dome, or many small domes. These stretch over the prayer hall and other rooms. The dome gives a feeling of space.

Hot air rises into the dome and helps to cool the mosque. The shape of the dome also makes sound travel, so everyone can hear the imam. Even though we have air-conditioning and microphones today, the dome helps to remind Muslims of how the first Muslims lived.

Courtyard

When this mosque was built, many people lived in small, crowded houses and did not have gardens. This courtyard was a cool, calm place for people to relax or talk to their friends. The fountain in the middle was used for washing before prayers.

This mosque was originally lit with oil lamps like this. Around the lamp are painted sayings from the **QUR'AN**. When the lamps were lit, the words would have been lit up.

9

Local mosques

A mosque is a building where Muslims go to pray, to learn and to be part of a community.

Is there a mosque in your neighbourhood? Have you ever visited a mosque? If you do, what you see might surprise you.

Outside the mosque

On the outside of the mosque you might see a **CRESCENT MOON** (picture ①). This is sometimes used as a symbol of Islam. Muslims use the Moon to find the times for important religious events and holidays.

You may also see **ARABIC** words on the outside of the mosque. Many Arabic words are used in Islam. This is because the first Muslims spoke Arabic and the holy book of Islam, called the **QUR'AN**, is in Arabic.

◀▲ ① Mosques often have pictures or sculptures of a Crescent Moon. The Crescent Moon is a symbol of Islam.

Many mosques have Arabic words on the outside. The words on this mosque mean Allah (God) and Mohammed (pbuh).

Weblink: www.CurriculumVisions.com/mosque

▶ ② This is the kind of mosque that you might see in your neighbourhood. It looks like an ordinary building because that is once what it was. Muslim people have not been in Britain long enough to build many mosques in a traditional style. So they have taken over other buildings and put them to sacred use.

▶ ③ This mosque was built in a very modern style. It is a large building because it also has classrooms, conference rooms and a bookshop.

Learning Arabic helps Muslims to understand the meaning of the Qur'an better.

What happens in a mosque

As you already know, a mosque is a place where Muslims pray together. But it is much more than that. Most mosques also have a school, where children and adults can take classes to learn about Islam or the Arabic language.

The mosque is also a community centre, where people gather for holiday celebrations, weddings or just to meet other Muslims.

Most mosques also have programmes where Muslims volunteer to help other Muslims in their neighbourhood and around the world.

No matter what size a mosque is, or what it looks like (pictures ② and ③), a lot happens at a mosque.

Learning and celebrating

A mosque is a place to learn about Islam, to celebrate and to meet other Muslims.

Study and learning are very important in Islam. Every Muslim is asked to learn as much about Islam as they can. This is done by studying the holy book called the Qur'an (picture ①). Almost every mosque has a school where children and adults can learn about Islam and the Arabic language.

In some mosques, classes may be held in the prayer hall (picture ②). The teacher and students might sit on the floor. Or there may be a separate room or building with classrooms, blackboards and a library like you have in school (picture ③).

A place to go for answers

Have you ever had a question or problem that you needed to ask someone about? Many Muslims come to the mosque to consult the imam about Islam in their daily life. The imam has studied all about Islam and can advise people when they have problems or questions about Islam.

▼ ① Mosques keep copies of the Qur'an and of other important Islamic books that discuss the Qur'an. Copies of the Qur'an, like this one, are often beautifully decorated to show how important they are.

▶ ② These children are studying in a special class at the mosque to memorise the Qur'an in Arabic. Memorising the entire Qur'an is very difficult, so anyone who does it is considered very intelligent.

Non-Muslims can also ask the imam if they have questions about Islam.

A place to celebrate

Have you ever been to a wedding or another celebration? Was it held in a religious building? Many Muslims choose to get married in a mosque (picture ④).

Muslims also gather at the mosque for Muslim celebrations like the **EID AL-FITR** and the **EID AL-ADHA**. On these days, there are special prayers. After the prayers, people may stay at the mosque to talk or to have a meeting.

▼ ③ A mosque is more than just a place to pray. These children are learning to use computers in a class at the mosque.

▼ ④ Many large mosques have rooms to hold classes and celebrations. This room is for festivals and wedding celebrations.

The mosque and the community

Your community is made up of people who you have something in common with. A mosque is an important part of every Islamic community.

A community may be made up of people who live, study, have the same interests or who worship in the same place.

Mosques give support

The centre of any Islamic community is the mosque because here any Muslim can always feel they can turn for guidance and support. For example, they can get help if they are very poor. It is also a place where people can meet, learn, sit and talk or just have a good time.

Because the mosque is part of the community, some mosques have places to eat and shops to buy religious books and pictures (pictures ① and ②).

The Islamic community

All Muslims belong to the worldwide Islamic community. Muslims call this worldwide community the UMMA. As a result, if a Muslim person is in a foreign country, they know they can always go to the nearest mosque to find help and guidance.

◀▲ ① This mosque has a cafeteria, where Muslims can gather to eat and talk after prayer. The cafeteria also provides free meals to poor Muslims in the community.

▼ ② **Many mosques have shops inside them that sell copies of the Qur'an, other Islamic books, or things like prayer beads and prayer mats.**

Rights and responsibilities

All Muslims have rights and responsibilities at the mosque. Some of the responsibilities include: observing the rules of the mosque, believing in certain things and praying in a special way.

The rights of going to a mosque include being able to go into a mosque at any time to have a quiet place to think and being able to pray free from any prejudice and stress.

Benefits

Muslims may get many benefits from going to a mosque. These may include: a chance to meet and make friends with other Muslims; having a place to celebrate; being able to learn more about Islam and the country your family came from; having a place to pray and having people to talk to about your concerns and problems.

15

One week at a mosque

A mosque has many regular events. Here are some of them.

Let's look at all the things that might happen at a mosque during one week.

There are activities and classes for everyone in the family. There are also activities such as the football club, that are not just about Islam.

Daily and Friday prayers

Muslims come to the mosque for one or more of the daily prayers if they can. Others pray at home, at work or at school.

Most important of all is the Friday midday prayer and SERMON (picture ①).

Evening classes and meetings

Depending on the size of the mosque, there may be evening classes and meetings for various groups. For example, our mosque has classes in Arabic, Islamic studies and cooking.

Many mosques also have meetings, such as women's meetings, and fundraising groups to help Muslims around the world.

Children's groups

Children often learn about Islam and Arabic at the mosque. So the mosque has classes and other activities for children. This is a way for children

▲ ① Muslims sometimes pray on their own, before group prayers begin.

who go to the mosque to meet and play with other Muslim children.

Differences

Each mosque has different activities and classes (picture ②). This is because each mosque is in a different community.

For example, a mosque in a neighbourhood with a lot of new immigrants might have many people who do not speak English as their first language. Some of these people might need extra help learning English.

Think about what your neighbourhood is like. If you went to a mosque in your neighbourhood, what kind of classes and activities would you expect it to have?

▼ ② A weekly timetable for a mosque. The time for prayers changes from day to day due to the change in time of sunrise and sunset.

Monday

4.53 a.m.	Prayer
1.22 p.m.	Prayer
2-4 p.m.	Infants' creche
4-5 p.m.	Arabic and Islamic studies for children
5.48 p.m.	Prayer
6-7.30 p.m.	Islamic studies for adults
7.30-9 p.m.	Arabic language for adults
9.51 p.m.	Prayer
11.21 p.m.	Prayer

Tuesday

4.52 a.m.	Prayer
1.22 p.m.	Prayer
2-4 p.m.	Infants' creche
3-5 p.m.	After-school children's club games and activities
7-8 p.m.	Women's programme: Islamic studies for women
8-9 p.m.	Fundraising meeting for the committee to help earthquake and famine victims in India and Africa.
5.49 p.m.	Prayer
9.52 p.m.	Prayer
11.22 p.m.	Prayer

Wednesday

4.52 a.m.	Prayer
1.22 p.m.	Prayer
1-2 p.m.	Weekly lunch for over 60s club
2-4 p.m.	Infants' creche
4-5 p.m.	Arabic and Islamic studies for children
5.49 p.m.	Prayer
7-8 p.m.	Cooking classes: the food of Punjab
8 p.m.	Weekly evening seminar. Tonight: local MP speaks about neighbourhood regeneration
9.53 p.m.	Prayer
11.23 p.m.	Prayer

Thursday

4.51 a.m.	Prayer
1.22 p.m.	Prayer
2-4 p.m.	Infants' creche
3-5 p.m.	After-school children's club games and activities
5-6 p.m.	English lessons
5.50 p.m.	Prayer
7-8 p.m.	Women's programme: reading the Qur'an
7-8 p.m.	Men's discussion group: interpreting the Qur'an
9.54 p.m.	Prayer
11.24 p.m.	Prayer

Friday

4.50 a.m.	Prayer
1.22 p.m.	Congregational prayer and sermon
5 p.m.	Volunteer group
5.50 p.m.	Prayer
7 p.m.	Women's programme: discussion group on Islamic issues
8 p.m.	Men's discussion group: Islamic issues
9.55 p.m.	Prayer
11.25 p.m.	Prayer

Saturday

4.50 a.m.	Prayer
1.23 p.m.	Prayer
1.30-3 p.m.	Football club for boys
1.30-3 p.m.	Football club for girls
5.51 p.m.	Prayer
8 p.m.	Islamic solidarity night: discussions and talks on Islam around the world. Tonight's speaker – an imam from the US talks about Islam in America
9.56 p.m.	Prayer
11.26 p.m.	Prayer

Sunday

4.49 a.m.	Prayer
1.23 p.m.	Prayer
10.30 -1.30 p.m.	Islamic weekend school: classes in Urdu, Islamic studies, Arabic and reading the Qur'an for children and adults
2-4 p.m.	Children's club: games and activities
4.30 -5.30 p.m.	Hajj meeting: planning and lessons for people who are going to make a pilgrimage to Mecca this year.
5.51 p.m.	Prayer
9.57 p.m.	Prayer
11.27 p.m.	Prayer

A visit to a mosque

The best way to learn about a mosque is to visit one. Before you can visit a mosque, you should know the rules and something about what you will see and do.

Visiting a religious building can be extremely interesting because it may be quite different from anything else you have seen.

What will we see and do at the mosque?

From the previous pages you should expect to see a prayer hall containing the minbar and the mihrab (picture ①). You will also see a place to wash. You may also see Arabic writing, a dome, an outdoor courtyard and one or more minarets.

Only Muslims may pray at a mosque, so you will not be visiting during prayers. Some of the things you may do at the mosque are: take your shoes off (picture ②); learn about how Muslims pray and ask questions. You can probably think

▼ ① These people are getting ready for prayers to begin.

▲ ② A rack for keeping shoes.

of many other things you will do at the mosque.

When you are inside the mosque, look for any features that you have learned about. If you see any Arabic writing, ask what it says (pictures ③ and ④). Notice the kind of decoration and art that is on the walls.

What is expected of you

You do not have to wear special clothes to visit a mosque, but you should dress in a way that shows respect. Girls should wear long sleeves.

Girls who are over 12 should also wear a scarf over their hair.

You do not have to whisper in a mosque. In fact, the people who show you around want you to ask questions! But you should act with respect.

▼ ③ Arabic writing and designs.

▲ ④ This writing on the inside of the dome lists some of the 99 descriptions of God. Some of these descriptions are "God the Merciful, God the Compassionate and God the all knowing."

Art in the mosque

Mosques are often decorated with beautiful art. The way a mosque is decorated tells us a lot about Islamic beliefs.

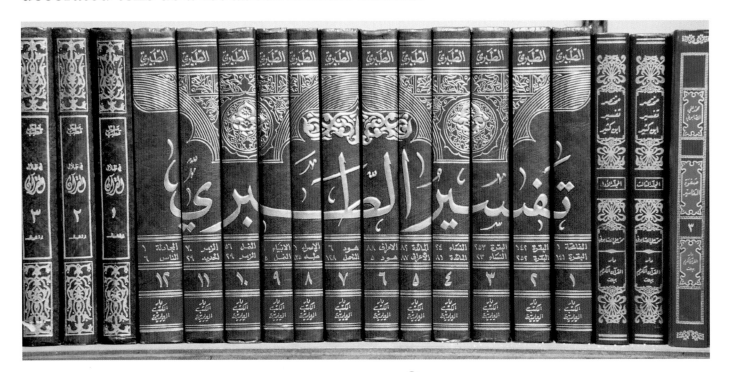

▲ ① Important Islamic books are sometimes decorated with designs and calligraphy to show how important they are. These are books about the Qur'an.

Most mosques have some kind of decoration. Muslims believe that it is wrong to worship pictures or statues, so there are no pictures or statues of people or animals inside a mosque. Instead, there might be beautiful geometric patterns and writing called CALLIGRAPHY.

Calligraphy

In calligraphy, letters and words are drawn in a beautiful and artistic way, so that the writing is also a kind of art. The calligraphy in these pictures are all from the Qur'an. You can see that there are many different styles of Arabic calligraphy.

Picture ① shows examples of some of the many different styles of Arabic calligraphy. Some types of calligraphy are plain and simple and other kinds are very complicated and fancy.

Calligraphy is a very important art in the Islamic world, because it is used to remind people of the beauty of the word of God.

Geometric designs

Instead of paintings or statues of people, mosques are often decorated with paintings or tiles of geometric designs (picture ②).

Because geometric patterns seem to go on forever, they help to remind people that God also goes on forever.

▲ ② Some mosques are painted with calligraphy and pictures of plants or geometric designs. The words on this painting mean "God is great."

▶ ③ Tiles from a mosque in Morocco.

Designs with flowers and plants are also popular. They look beautiful and help to remind people of the garden of paradise they will find in heaven.

Tiles

Mosques in the past were often decorated with tiles. The tiles looked beautiful and they also lasted much longer than paint. Mosques today are sometimes decorated with tiles as part of this tradition (picture ③).

Wood carvings

Inside a mosque you may see carved wooden screens. These are called mashrabiyyas. If you stand behind a mashrabiyya screen, you can see other people but they cannot see you. Women sometimes pray behind the screens so they can see out but no one can see them.

Mosques around the world

There are mosques in every country around the world. They all have some things in common, and some differences. Let's visit some and find out why.

Wherever they are, and however they look, all mosques still have some things in common, like the prayer hall. But every Muslim community around the world has a different culture and history. So, mosques around the world often look different (pictures ① and ②).

◀ ① An ancient mosque, the Blue Mosque, Istanbul, Turkey, made from stone.

▶ ② A modern mosque in the Middle Eastern country of Dubai.

This is very noticeable, for example, in China, where some mosques were built in the style of traditional Chinese pagodas (picture ③).

Mosques built from local materials

Many mosques have been built from the most common local building materials. Around the world, you can find mosques built of stone, brick, mud, wood and cement.

Modern mosques

Many mosques built in the last 100 years or so have been built using modern materials and styles. Many modern mosques may not look like traditional mosques – but they still have all the features of traditional mosques (picture ④).

▼ ④ This mosque in Jakarta, Indonesia, is one of the world's largest.

▼ ③ The minaret in this mosque is built like a pagoda. It is in Xian, China.

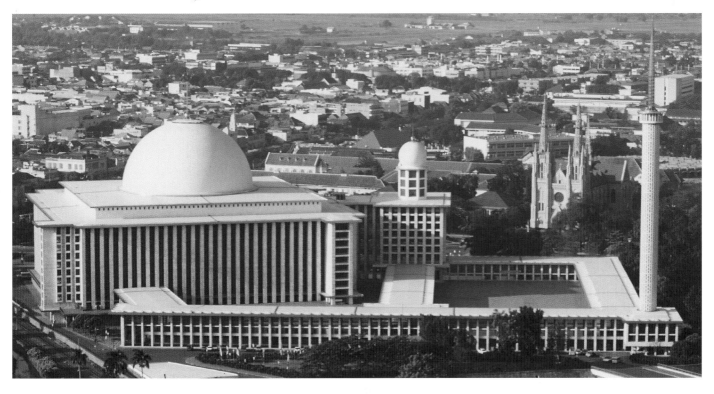

23

Index

Curriculum Visions

Curriculum Visions is a registered trademark of Atlantic Europe Publishing Company Ltd.

Atlantic Europe Publishing

Teacher's Guide
There is a Teacher's Guide to accompany this book, available only from the publisher.

Dedicated Web Site
There's more about other great Curriculum Visions packs and a wealth of supporting information available at our dedicated web site:

www.CurriculumVisions.com

First published in 2003 by
Atlantic Europe Publishing Company Ltd
Copyright © 2003
Atlantic Europe Publishing Company Ltd

Authors
Lisa Magloff, BA and Brian Knapp, BSc, PhD
Religious Adviser
Imam Abdul Kadee Shafiq
Art Director
Duncan McCrae, BSc
Editor
Gillian Gatehouse
Senior Designer
Adele Humphries, BA
Acknowledgements
The publishers would like to thank the following for their help and advice: East London Mosque; Central London Mosque; Suleymaniye Mosque.

Photographs
The Earthscape Editions photolibrary except page 22 top left: Serena Temperley.
Illustrations
David Woodroffe
Designed and produced by
Earthscape Editions
Reproduced in the Czech Republic by
Global Colour sro
Printed in Hong Kong by
Wing King Tong Company Ltd

Mosque – *Curriculum Visions*
A CIP record for this book is available from the British Library

Paperback ISBN 1 86214 303 X
Hardback ISBN 1 86214 305 6

This product is manufactured from sustainable managed forests. For every tree cut down at least one more is planted.